Vivian Smith | Here, There and Elsewhere

New Poems

Vivian Smith

GIRAMONDO POETS

Here, There and Elsewhere

First Published 2012
from the Writing & Society Research Centre
at the University of Western Sydney
by the Giramondo Publishing Company
PO Box 752 Artarmon NSW 1570 Australia
www.giramondopublishing.com

Designed by Harry Williamson
Typeset by Andrew Davies
In 10/16.5 pt Baskerville

Printed and bound by Ligare Book Printers
Distributed in Australia by NewSouth Books

National Library of Australia
Cataloguing-in-Publication data:

Vivian Smith 1933 –
Here, There and Elsewhere / Vivian Smith
9781920882815 (pbk.)
A821.3

for Sybille

Other poetry collections by Vivian Smith

The Other Meaning
An Island South
Familiar Places
Tide Country
Selected Poems
New Selected Poems
Late News
Along the Line

Acknowledgements

Poems in this collection have previously appeared in *Antipodes*, *Australian Book Review*, *HEAT*, *Meanjin*, *Quadrant*, *Snorkel* and *La Traductière*, as well as in several volumes of the annual *Best Australian Poems* (Black Inc) and are here brought together for the first time.

I am particularly grateful to Ivor Indyk for *HEAT* which has made such a difference to writing in Australia over the last fifteen years.

This project has been assisted by the Commonwealth Government through the Australia Council, its art funding and advisory body.

Contents

The Real Life of Ern Malley

Poems found among the papers of the lamented writer

The silent work

The silent work of uneventful days
burst on the world that dismal afternoon.
Max and his crowd had their funny ways.
I at least knew how to sing in tune.

I needed my revenge. I was ignored.
My good work was constantly rejected.
I like my enemies completely floored.
I'd show them what it means to be respected.

Ethel got it wrong. I disappeared.
I gave up writing years ago, in dread.
Poems couldn't hide the things I feared.
Wahre Kunst ist kalt, as Schoenberg said.

I laughed out loud to see Max in a mess,
gracious in victory, serene with success.

The grand cham

The grand cham of our Australian verse,
that leather jacket, those neat jeans,
declared me out of bounds and sick and worse,
one of the perpetual has beens.

Life was so restricted in those days.
We had to knuckle down and earn our keep.
But I wrote poems even in my sleep,
knowing that I needed no one's praise.

Time out, on the sidelines: that was fine.
I was never part of any scene,
the notion even seemed a bit obscene,

but I was free, alive, and in my prime,
and went on pulling poems from my hat,
none of them predictable or pat.

Parrots in paintings

for Sidney Nolan and Albert Tucker

Parrots in paintings was my theme.
I had three hundred slides and ninety cards.
To be a man of letters was my dream,
the history of art in our backyards.

I wrote them all down. It was just for you:
Manet, Courbet, the Expressionists,
August Macke and Max Liebermann.
The way they did each beak. Such mannerists!

What is it about parrots, sage old birds,
who speak to us across the centuries,
asking for a biscuit in three words,
dancing on a perch instead of trees?

They try to stare us out, can even scoff:
go figure, strange man, bugger off.

You couldn't be

You couldn't be a homo in the '40s:
no place in this town for blokes like you.
But I was one whom labels didn't fit
and went on paddling my canoe.

Had I lost my way, or just not found it,
living in a puzzling in-between?
Something always trying to confound it,
dabbling in a world of might have been.

I wanted to escape falsity
and not become a well-known public figure,
to take my time and loaf beneath my tree,
not always with my finger on the trigger.

I had to stand alone. I had no team.
Beneath the civil surface slept the scream.

I lived with those

I lived with those who did not know the truth
and tried to save my life from life's mess,
a damaged man, I never wore a dress,
but soon became obsessed with passing youth.

I took a job in an outback garage.
I like my writing finished, not too raw:
after one oasis, the mirage.
Art flourishes and follows its own law.

I envied other people's happiness.
I hated squeaky wheels who tried like Max
to rule the roost and all its journo hacks.

They never know they never know enough
but live on crowing in a world of bluff,
pretentious wankers claiming they are tough.

Ethel got it wrong

Ethel got it wrong deliberately.
She muddled up the few facts she had found.
Ern was never in the underground,
he disappeared and lived on quietly

the backwater life he needed.
A wartime job, mechanical repairs.
A barracks room and half a dozen stairs.
I want to be alone, that's all, he pleaded.

Ern had always thought that he was gay
and couldn't bear the shame and the distress.
He felt he had to lock himself away

but finally risked all for happiness.
No one was into sex and snorting then
but Ern knew how he felt about young men.

He wore his hair

He wore his hair in different shades of green –
an episode he lived to regret.
To be born old and never seventeen
is not a fact you easily forget.

Something then was following its course,
emerging like an awkward adolescent.
His poems wanted to be evanescent
but trim and spare and balancing their force.

Something seemed to be taking its time,
it had a secret message it would send,
he only had to wait his turn in line,
certain it would get there in the end.

And yes, he knew then, standing in the rain,
he'd never keep such company again.

Sidney's portrait

Sidney's portrait of a shitting dog
has just been auctioned for a million dollars.
It shows a small group round a boree log,
a drover's wife decked out in greens and yellows.

Or that was how it looked in '42.
Today we read it in such varied ways:
Pig Iron Bob glaring from a shoe
and Japs approaching through the Moreton Bays.

The figure in the woodpile's neat display
that seems to snigger as it thumbs its nose,
is Max at Heide – seen the other way
it's Ern just turning – so the story goes.

Of course it all looks different today
and paintings say what only paintings say.

Diary without Dates

On voit et on rêve – FLAUBERT

I used to meet her

I used to meet her walking down the street,
one of the best minds of her generation,
sometimes with a dog, sometimes alone,
later with a nurse, a paid sister.

Strange to see that blank evaporation.
I thought of all her books, her safe career,
chairs in Sydney, Paris and Toulouse,
and then the silence, how it just descended.

Remember Alec Hope in his last years,
a poet without poems left to write,
and Iris Murdoch slowly losing it,
among the best minds of their generation.

Trying to keep ourselves in working order
hoping to escape complete attrition.

My old school

Prorsum et semper honeste

My old school is now a funeral parlour:
I stand and stare in disbelief and wonder –
that pink façade, those 1916 bricks –
where I survived from '45 to '50,
one war ending, others just beginning
the year my parents' marriage fell apart
and left me floating free and floundering,
a mixture of timidity and cheek.
The time snow fell and stayed around a week.

Maugham and Greene and later Joyce and Kafka,
erotics of a face and a physique,
times when soul and body came together,
wild as Rimbaud, feeble as Verlaine,
and first poems looking for direction.

These wayside shrines

These wayside shrines, these flower-encumbered altars
that spring up overnight on highway corners
a fist of wattle fastened to a pole,
an empty bottle with a withered rose,
an ornate orchid broken in a pot
mark the spot to show us where it happened.
They hurt like grief with head bowed at the roadside.

I've stood in Lower Austria and Spain
at crossroads where a crucifix appears
carved by worn and awkward peasant hands,
and read old shrines in gardens in Japan
bearing gifts imploring the unknown –
propitiations that I see are prayers.

A Paris Morning

A Paris morning, fifty years ago,
Cocteau's homage to Apollinaire
as he unveiled Picasso's *Muse's Head*.
Too late, I almost missed it all
in the small square right next to St Germain.
A photojournalist still lingered on
snapping up the disappearing moment.

And there it stood, a head upon a plinth,
as if it meant to have its portrait painted,
a muse figure staring into space,
Cocteau elegant in light grey suit.
And as I looked he turned and drifted off
floating towards the crowded boulevard.

Desiderata

The programme talks about her damaged life,
the way the dream led towards her poems.
She lived on another planet in Kashmir,
her photo featured in the TV guide.

I think, God what a life and what a cost,
are any poems worth the price she paid?
Am I mishearing what the programme says?

Birds are up to small tricks in the garden.

The stoic life for me, my times decided,
no needles then, no way to get away.

How one-dimensional their phrases sound,
friends and slogans from another day.

I saw them marching once, stoned crowds,
Free the weed and *Join us in the clouds.*

Paul Éluard in Sydney

Disparaître c'est réussir

In 1924, at a time of personal crisis when some of his Surrealist friends had decided to give up writing, Paul Éluard disappeared from Paris on a round the world voyage which gave him a port of call in Sydney.

They are such witty bastards, all those guys.
I left them to their tight artistic scene,
flummoxed by the questions they can't answer.
Success means disappearing from their screen.

Tristesse drives me through the slack *tropiques,*
a friendship shattered and a lover lost.
A first class journey to review my life
and only I know how to count the cost.

Some good will come of this or I'll jump ship
and do a Rimbaud, follow sea and sky.

Sumatra, source of camphor, passes by;
plumbago is completely Ceylonese.

They're either red or blue these southern trees.
Poems start to catch me by surprise.

Images, fragments

Others have their documents, their trees,
their family records clear. It all rings true.
They know where they come from and where they're heading.
For them the gate is straight and they push through.

All I have are images: your house,
music on a table in the hall,
photos of the Royal Family
and Edith Cavell waiting on the wall

and two paintings that you must have loved,
Leighton's *Wedded* in a big brown frame,
a gilded oval called *The Sea Hath Pearls*
by some painter of forgotten name.

Then the blank, the shutters clattered down
and kindness started in another town.

In the Butterfly House, Vienna

I expected silk and colour, old brocade,
exotic palpitations, streaks of gold,
rosenkavaliers flirting in the shade,
but suddenly the day turned cold.

Was this the wrong time, or the wrong year,
a switch forgotten yesterday?
A few were starting to cause fear,
cloth that flutters as it rots away,

and several had an eyepatch on each wing,
drawing to repel admiration,
staring one way, flying off the other

wanting to be thought some other thing.
One tried an occasional gyration –
call it a final fling, brother.

October 2007: in dürftiger Zeit

I could become a cranky mad old man
shouting in a temper, kicking up a fuss,
or else display sarcastic perfect manners,
'can't complain', 'musn't grumble' me.

I've always tried to make the best of things,
to find a diet in a can of worms.
The bleakest introspection haunts my days
but there's no way I'd ever let you know it.

Trees are stressed and nibbled to the quick
in this old suburb not far up the line.
The experts say this time of drought will pass,
churches waiting with their prayers for rain.

Slogans fade on cars: *Lest we forget,*
Save the rainforests, Free Tibet.

Train to Leura

The train to Leura early Sunday morning
and our compartment full of total strangers,
Russian-speaking hikers, boots and shorts,
and four Americans, I'd say, late sixties,
calling out the stations as they pass:
'Melbourne was more interesting than this',
'The trees looked better across Portugal.'
'I want to see a kangaroo today'.
They tick the names off on their tourist map,
and every twenty minutes of our trip
'I've still not seen a single kangaroo'.
I feel like saying and you will not see
a single emu now at Emu Plains,
but that would take me too long to explain.

I like these chatting couples, so relaxed:
they say exactly what they want to say,
they care, and do not care, they laugh out loud,
'I've still not seen a single kangaroo',
the two behind them chomping on their snacks,
sliced carrots, polished Packham pears.

Understanding

The painter was an understated man,
he said so little, always seemed remote,
his portraits melancholy and austere.
He never told the viewer what to think:
a woman standing near a kitchen sink,
a young girl with a letter in her hand
said ‘I see’ and meant ‘I understand’.

At last his story starts to get around:
the problem was the parents, not the child.
He grew a silent rebel, hidden, mild,
his only friend for years a small white dog.

The critics then declared they’d found the clue:
the open door said no, the wall refused
to toe the line or do what others do –
clear at last they knew what was who.

Remembering a friend

And then you felt you had to get away
and write in silence, with your favourite book
Insect Wonders of Australia.
Your work survives and shows what once existed.

Your regime lasted through those final years –
off on Friday nights, in town by Tuesday:
'Give me useful lies, not harmful truths.
I'm on the look out now for consolations'.

You never played it safe though you pretended
that you preferred a wild colonial garden
to tufts of mondo grass, a patch of pebbles,
or pushing rocks up slopes to make a terrace.

You scorned the gods and lived without the myths
until a fire turned it all to ashes.

Brennan 1932

These are the streets through which the poet wandered,
an old man in the ruin of his life,
remembering the talents slowly squandered,
the futile strife.

A wrong turning with a long lost key,
a path abandoned, and then misremembered:
pressed he'd simply say he couldn't say,
overconfident and too encumbered.

But poems still survived his early search
resisting one long series of defeats;
he sat for solace in this quiet church,
shades of Lilith lurking in the streets,
dreaming of the paper worlds he made
and offerings to Venus in a glade.

Rereading the biography

I like the early years the best –
that time of pinch and scrape and work and struggle.
I care much less now for the public figure,
the wild man who died so full of fame.
Tittle-tattle, back-biting, slander, jealousy.

The limited success, the lack of mess,
before the festivals and the big launches.
Par délicatesse, j'ai perdu ma vie.

Sometimes he'd watch a sparrow flutter in
an inch of water showing miles of sky,
or save a bee or butterfly from drowning,
too late of course to turn its life around,
though some things could be managed in small doses.
Never forgot a kindness or a friend.

The Monument

Commissioned by Mrs Agnes Hamilton-Grey

So this is where they put her monument
in 1940, Sydney sandstone too,
her tribute to the poet she adored:
'I tread the air and scrutinise the sun',
a careful quote from Aristophanes,
weather-worn, half-hidden under trees.

Our last colonial poet, what a story,
his fern gullies flattened, drained away.
He speaks to us of mortal hope and failure;
no one spares his monument a glance.

She hungered all her life for quality,
obsessed with recognition and survival.
An ibis seems to look at me askance,
a headline glares *Another boat arrival.*

My Island

Your name crops up in unexpected places,
in poems dropped by Valéry Larbaud
and books by Nabokov and Mark Twain.
Jack London took a photograph of you,
loafing with his arms around a woman.
Cendrars made the best of things.

Some arrived and simply disappeared
like artists in their paintings and their poems,
pissed off by the wholly local scene,
or drank themselves to death around the wharves
waiting for the boat that never came,
or set up neat boutiques – the tourist trade.
Others retreated into cheap hotels
writing articles on clarinets and snails.

A Garden in Van Diemen's Land

This walled garden was the one she loved,
speaking to the Europe of her mind.
It faced the sun with such serene composure.
For those who made it, it was just a grind.

The cruelty of plant life still disturbed her,
the way they use, abuse, and fight each other,
compete for food, for space in which to flourish,
rising up by knocking others down.
They cannot thrive without control and order.
They need the lash, the stake, the guiding twine.

Beauty is a question of appearance,
assurance of the lily, the pertinacious rose
the ivy covets with its cool embrace,
and every flower must settle in its place.

Phone Call

i.m. Gary Catalano

'Still fossicking in old anthologies,
sifting through abandoned realms of gold?',
you ring to say hullo and tell me how
you've found another group of the erased,
writers who stood alone, who speak for all.

'To recover for our time their qualities,
to see at last a kind of justice done
for other ways of looking at the world,
precise observation, unforced tone.'

Your voice is light with late discoveries.
I tell you of the long slog I have made
through volumes overlooked and underrated.
'Five years work now coming to an end
and every new discovery a gift'.

We talked of this, and that, and letting go,
your new binoculars, your morning walk
to watch some fox cubs playing down the road –

that was our last phone call. I remember.

Postcards from Capri

to Desmond O'Grady

Villa Discopoli 1907

A whole winter free at last for work,
space and time that I can call my own,
and in this clear productive atmosphere
flourish like an aloe all alone.

Outside the coasts of Magna Graecia,
wind in the pines and years since I decided
to live in simple silence like a monk
obedient to the rules that I've elided.

So I begin with basic exercises
translating *Sonnets from the Portuguese*
like someone in a church on bended knees
fiddling with a string of worn-out beads,
searching for the sense of what is real,
the truth of what I am and what I feel.

Zum Kater Hiddigeigei 1913

A title sells a movement like a book:
dynamism, electricity!
Give me engines and the world of speed,
trams and trains and aeroplanes and cars.

I want to see all libraries in flame,
museums and academies in ruin,
and let me see a cinema erected
where once an old cathedral dominated.

I know I hold the future in my hand.

Give me city squares and public spaces,
halls, domains, platforms, intersections
where I can shout my simple truth out loud.
I want to be the leader of a crowd.

How many fresh starts is one man allowed?

Casa Malaparte 2010

The house is cool and beautiful today,
a temple to the sun, a flight of stairs,
a landing pad, a runway to the sea
in weather worn and deep Pompeian red,
an act of calm and ultimate defiance,
as much a statement as a planned retreat,
the place that Rommel wanted, Yanks adored –
you left the lot to China in the end.

Your writing flourished in the shifting sands
of Fascist Italy and World War II
with Europe led to ruins by its saviours.

An awkward figure at the best of times,
you saw the death of all the gods you fought for,
and nothing now remains of you but art.

Streets of Hobart and Elsewhere

Carrying Tanguy up the Stairs

Tasmania's French connections survive in maps, monuments and books. All those explorers who nearly made the island French rather than British have left their names from the D'Entrecasteaux Channel to Freycinet Peninsula, and monographs and articles record their impact and influence. In the 1950s these connections took on a new lease of life when the French Polar Exploration ships used to moor at Hobart on their way to and from Adélie Land in the Antarctic, and for a week the streets of Hobart would be dotted with red pompoms as *matelots* made their way around the shops or queued up in the post office. It was probably because of these visits that Hobart was chosen to be the first port of call for the most important exhibition of paintings to come to Australia since the end of the Second World War.

In 1952 I had been studying French language and literature for several years and was discovering French painting. Although I was always intensely interested in Tasmanian and Australian history and culture, my intellectual appetite was larger than my surroundings could satisfy and I was turning more and more to the European rather than the local for added sustenance. Just before Christmas I was told that a large collection of modern French paintings was going to visit Hobart on its way to Sydney, an exhibition that might well be the forerunner of many others. No one had any idea what it would contain, apart from a Picasso and a Matisse or two, but there was a sense of excitement and anticipation. One Tasmanian art student told me she thought this might well change her whole life. The exhibition, which was coming by ship from Melbourne, was to open in mid-January 1953. I was asked to stay around in case help was needed and told that there might be interesting people to meet. One of the features of life in a place like Hobart, which had all the advantages of being a capital city as well as all the qualities of a small town, was that you could get to see and meet nearly everyone who came there, especially in the world of the arts.

On Boxing Day the *Mercury* announced that the freighter which was bringing the paintings to Hobart had run aground on a sandbar near Wineglass Bay on the East Coast and that no one saw any way of freeing it.

You can imagine the shock. The Christmas/New Year season can be a particularly difficult one in Tasmanian waters, which are unpredictable at any time. One year a huge school of whales had been washed ashore and left stranded at Marion Bay. Another year two yachtsmen were washed overboard and drowned. A family friend had recently lost his life fishing off Betsy Island near the Iron Pot. The poetry of Baudelaire, Mallarmé and Rimbaud in particular had made me aware of how maritime disasters could image the uncertain and the unforeseeable. Literature and life! And here was a coastal freighter in the 1950s, on what should have been a routine voyage between two states, caught on a sandbar with an irreplaceable collection of paintings as its cargo.

Today of course TV stations would carry the news; helicopters would be hovering over the scene with on-the-spot reports. In those days there were only brief radio announcements, and you had to wait for the one and only morning paper with its monopoly on the news to bring the latest information.

Le Tout-Hobart was aghast and agog with the news. Nobody knew what exactly had happened. Had there been too much Christmas celebration aboard? Had the captain been drunk? These were questions that no one asked aloud but in the rolling of an eye or the lift of an eyebrow. So far as I know no investigation was held into the cause of the mishap. There were 119 paintings aboard, many by world-famous artists, and there was widespread fear that they could be damaged, or destroyed. Their fate became international news. Lloyds of London had to finance the salvaging operation. When it was at last ascertained that the paintings were at least safe, there was the further fear that Hobart might miss out on the exhibition altogether, as it was travelling to a tight schedule. Finally, after nearly two weeks' delay, it was decided to off-load the whole collection. The paintings were safely landed and brought to Hobart by road.

The exhibition was held upstairs in the Tasmanian Museum and Art Gallery, which one entered in those days from the steps near the corner of Argyle Street. The afternoon the paintings arrived in Hobart I was asked with a couple of student friends to help with the installation. The official opening by the French Consul from Melbourne was to take place the next day. Everything was running late and as much assistance as possible was needed. It too was a case of all hands on deck.

Many of the items were heavy and bulky, including four remarkable tapestries: Dufy's *The Beautiful Summer*, Gromaire's *The Earth*, Jean Lurçat's *Tapestry of the Great Fear* and Henri Matisse's wonderful Beauvais tapestry of 1947–48, *Polynesia*. These powerful works must have been carried in and installed by the contractors who had transported all the material from St Helens on the East Coast under the watchful eye of a descendant of the Pissarro family who was in charge of the whole enterprise. But much of the exhibition consisted of medium-sized paintings, some small enough to be carried by one person, others best carried by two.

I have recently consulted the catalogue again and been reminded of the titles of some of the smaller items displayed. There were pieces by Georges Braque, Marc Chagall, André Derain and three buoyant Dufys.

Bernard Buffet, who was probably the youngest painter in the exhibition, was represented by a very recent work of 1949 entitled *The Painter*. Max Ernst had a visionary, futuristic piece *The Year 1955*; and there were lively pieces by Dunoyer de Segonzac, Fernand Léger, André Lhote, Miró, Picabia and Picasso. These paintings were not the major achievements of these artists – and indeed the exhibition included artists heard of neither before nor since – but the fact that it was a survey introducing representative names was part of its great value and success.

There were some extraordinary works. Matisse's tapestry *Polynesia* is unforgettable, with its starfish and stars and shells and its lapping underwater blue and tropical white, and Jean Lurçat's Aubusson *Tapestry of the Great Fear* with its leaf and night sky pattern seemed from one angle to dominate the whole room. It was an introduction to an aspect of art that I at nineteen had never encountered. Georges Rouault, with his stained-glass religious figures and social outcasts, remained one of my main personal discoveries from the collection. I had recently been absorbed in the poetry of David Gascoyne and his translations of Pierre Jean Jouve had led me on to the originals (a few years later I saw the poet himself at a lecture in his honour at the Sorbonne) and at one stage I planned an article on the affinity between the poems of Jouve and the paintings of Rouault – a project that did not exactly evaporate, but which still remains in note form in a folder full of other unrealised schemes. There was a Nicolas de Staël composition in thick squares of colour, a typical Utrillo scene, a Vlaminck of haystacks which could have been painted near Richmond or Pontville, Jacques Villon orange trees and a view of mountains by Zao Wou-Ki.

It amazes me to recall that I carried or helped to carry these paintings up the stairs with my bare hands – a Buffet, a Miró and a Vlaminck up the stairs – actually holding them in my hands and helping to hang them on a special hessian frame set up in the room. When I see all the elaborate and necessary safeguards and precautions that are now part of hanging an exhibition, I am astonished at the simple unprofessionalism with which we helped set up this show. There was a moment of hilarity when it was discovered that some of the workmen had arranged one of the pictures sideways, and someone laughed about artists who had merely framed their palettes. 'Take your foot out of that Matisse' a voice shouted as I stepped back to see if the painting I had hung was at the right angle. Of course it was only a joke, but a fair amount of nervous tension built up in the room during the few hours we were there, and again and again the position of certain pictures had to be altered. It was an experience never to be repeated and, in one sense, the closest I have ever been to such famous works. The last painting I helped to carry up the stairs was the one that came to haunt me most.

I have never really much cared for the paintings of Yves Tanguy. His sandscapes full of speckled pebbles and other lunar lolly shapes struck me as curiously inert and lifeless. His 'Dark Garden' (*Le Jardin Sombre*) of 1927 is an oddly arid work but it seems to have fed into a strange series of dreams that I experienced at the time. In one my hands became a huge volcanic landscape full of extinct craters and leprous pits, and as I peered down to look closer over a cliff edge, I seemed to plunge and float into a cloudscaped night sky full of sand and ashes. It was a dream that oppressed me for days in what I used to think of as my surrealist phase, and while it was quite probably caused by my excessive smoking – I was practically a chain-smoker at the time – that dream landscape was clearly informed by some of the images in the paintings in the exhibition, particularly the Tanguy.

The exhibition by the painters of the *École de Paris* came at the beginning of a lifelong passion that has continued undiminished. My self-education in art up to that time owed nearly everything to picture postcards, Penguin Prints, Penguin Modern Painters, King Penguins and the Faber Gallery, as well as to *Art in Australia*. Like places and monuments I had never visited but knew only from photographs, I had already acquired a wide knowledge of numerous works of art and I could recognise them from reproductions. I found it extraordinarily moving to be seeing at first hand paintings by artists whose work I had only seen in prints. I had not yet read Walter Benjamin's essay on 'The Work of Art in the Age of Mechanical Reproduction' or André Malraux's *Les Voix du Silence*, both of which emphasise the uniqueness of the presence of the original work of art itself. The notion of the aura that surrounds, or even the radiance that emanates from, the original object has its problems, but I have certainly experienced what Keats calls the 'pure serene' that fills one in the presence of a masterpiece and I think that I felt something of that in front of Dufy's beguiling *Still Life with Bananas* and Joan Miró's shapely *Penguin* and his other painting, *Forty-Eight*, which, like so many of the pieces in the exhibition was a glimpse into the future, focused on the perfectly drawn number 48.

Of course the exhibition contained work that was puzzling; some of it haunting and troubling. I was an inexperienced viewer. Among the many landscapes, still lives, factory and farm scenes, flower pieces, homages to predecessors, abstract compositions, portraits and nudes, there were paintings that I looked at not knowing what to do with what I saw. I had only a few reference points, and no way of knowing whether some of the things I saw were good or bad of their kind. But even the unformulated doubts and uncertainties that I must have felt eventually proved fruitful in unexpected ways.

The show met with various reactions in Hobart, but my general impression was one of excitement, curiosity and a sense of pleasure at the chance to see work which would otherwise have not been available to us in those years. Everybody I knew went to see it, some several times, and people seemed to go on talking about it for months. Then, soon after the exhibition moved from Hobart to Sydney, well-known members of the old guard like Howard Ashton and Norman Lindsay started attacking it and all that they claimed it stood for. 'An Emetic in Oil Paint', Norman Lindsay was reported as saying.

I did not then know enough about Norman Lindsay to realise how predictable his reaction was, or how the *Bulletin* with which he had such close connections would use his outburst for its own publicity purposes.

In time I would learn more about the various strands that go to make up the web of Australian culture. In those years Hobart seemed to be full of post-war migrants (collectively referred to as 'the Balts') who were to have such an impact over the following decades. I was getting to know some of them as I had got to know some of the refugees who had first arrived in the late '30s. Slowly I discovered that there is a current in Australian culture which always reacts and warns against foreigners and outside and overseas influences, fearing corruption. It is represented at both ends of the political spectrum: on the one hand by the reactionary attitudes of Norman Lindsay and his circle; on the other by the Utopian poetic visions of Bernard O'Dowd. I discovered it again in Kenneth Mackenzies' novel *The Refuge* which appeared a year after the French Exhibition, and which I read at the time as an allegory of 'young Australia' being seduced by impure old-world Europe. I certainly did not think that Australian artists should uncritically imitate whatever was the latest international fashion, but that they should learn from and make what use they could of what was brought to them from overseas; that there should be constant fruitful interaction to combat entropy and stagnation.

The 1953 exhibition of French paintings was ultimately as important for Australian painting as the pre-war Melbourne *Herald* exhibition had been. Recently published artists' diaries like those of Judy Cassab and John Olsen confirm the sense of excitement, innovation and discovery that the exhibition brought with it; and it is a fact that the Tasmanian painters Jack Carrington Smith and Rosamond McCulloch, to mention only two, became much more experimental in their work after the 1953 exhibition. Bernard Smith in his history of Australian painting singles out its importance for Australian painting as a whole. And there is a fine record of the show in the series of photographs that Max Dupain made of it in Sydney.

Much later in the year the French/Australian newspaper *Le Courier Australien* featured half a dozen poems by Ray Mathew, all based on various paintings in the exhibition. Mathew was one of the most widely published young writers in Australia at the time and the verse he was producing showed the ease and fluency with which he could take up a subject and develop it lightly and loosely. Much of his writing was a kind of lyrical journalism and the best of it had an attractive freshness and warmth. When I read his poems in *Le Courier Australien* I remember wondering why I had not been moved to write something similar. After all, I had personally held some of those paintings in my arms. Images from one or two seemed to have entered into my dreams. But I had not felt impelled to write poems about them.

When I met Mathew for the first time in Sydney a little later, he asked me if I had started to write poems about Sydney, full of my first impressions. I said I didn't usually write poems while I was travelling about and that I probably needed to get back to the isolation of my room at home. He seemed astonished and said he got worried if he didn't write something every day and hated going a week without having a complete poem to show. This impressed me no end but I somehow realised that whatever happened that would not, could not, be my way.

The Three Houses of Pablo Neruda

I always enjoy museums and art galleries and rarely miss an opportunity to visit one, but I only go looking for writers' houses (which can contain elements of both) if I feel a special liking for the work and its creator, or curiousity about the life. The little chateau of Muzot above Sierre where Rilke completed the *Duino Elegies* and wrote the *Sonnets to Orpheus* in one of the greatest transports of inspiration in the history of literature; Robert Louis Stevenson's Vailima above the harbour at Apia in Samoa, Virginia Woolf's modest Monk's House, Rodmell, and Henry James's more imposing but unostentatious Lamb House at Rye are among the most memorable I have seen. None of these has moved me quite as much as Barbara Hepworth's beautiful studio and garden at St Ives in Cornwall, with its view across church tower and slate rooftops to fishing boat masts, harbour and bay. And no writer's house has struck me quite as forcibly as those of Pablo Neruda, which have now become national monuments, preserved by an independent foundation which protects them from the vagaries of changes of government and fashion as part of the National Heritage of Chile. When I saw them last year I had the impression that they had been carefully lifted out of the political into the world of the *musée imaginaire*.

The Latin American republics have an unusual

record in relation to their most famous writers. A number of French authors – Claudel, Saint-John Perse, Giraudoux – were trained and experienced diplomats, but Rubén Darío, Gabriela Mistral, Alfonso Reyes, Pablo Neruda and Octavio Paz were appointed to diplomatic posts by their countries because they were poets and as a reward and incentive for being writers, which was presumably taken to indicate highly educated and administratively competent. Certainly the records seem to prove that they carried out their responsibilities with skill and flair even if a few of them had notable fallings out with their governments or changes of regime. Impossible to imagine an Australian government appointing Judith Wright or A. D. Hope to such positions, even if it is equally unlikely that either would have accepted such a post. The late Gardner Davies, the noted Mallarmé scholar, was given a sinecure as cultural attaché at the Australian Embassy in Paris for many years. J. R. Rowland was a life-long diplomat and there are now several poets who work in the department of External Affairs, but Australia has no record of recognition in this area.

Neruda had three houses built or converted for him in the later years of his life from the money acquired from his published work and international prizes, to mark his profound attachment to the country of his birth after years of exile and life abroad. All were intended to be left to the people of Chile rather than as monuments to himself. All are highly individual and well worth visiting both for their own sake and for the glimpse they seem to give into some aspects of the poetry. All command superb views and outlooks. Each one makes an impression of robust vigour; rather plain looking, colourful on the outside but playful, self-indulgent and warmly welcoming inside, perhaps with a touch of self-importance or mockery. All three contain collections of exquisite objects – rows and rows of glass paperweights and wine goblets, boxes of seashells, glass cases of butterflies and insects, but there is nothing finicky or precious about the houses themselves, which rather recall ships with rooms like cabins, and spiral stairs that suggest descent into boiler or engine rooms. All of the houses are portioned out into a series of separate smaller rooms or annexes and have the sense of proportion one associates with luxury yachts or small cruisers. Everything is comfortably ship-shape and in place.

Neruda's house in Santiago, La Chascona, carefully restored after the pillaging and looting it suffered in the days following Pinochet's overthrow of the Allende regime, is in the Bellavista area, not far from the zoo, in a small, very attractive artistic street that reminds one of similar corners in other parts of the world – say a side street in Hampstead or Montparnasse – but with its own unique Spanish and Chilean colonial touches: inner courtyard, ceramic tiles, small wall fountain.

Once in the door and up the stairs, out of the dazzling heat of the day, the shape and design of the house start to open out. The whole is built as a series of bungalows or studios on a cliffside slope, new sections added over the years when Neruda could afford it, and organised around a central garden space. Next to the front office is a long dining room and bar: Neruda was a great lover of the fruits of the earth, a *bon viveur* and a connoisseur of food and wine which he so often celebrated in his writing. Throughout his life he collected coloured wine-glasses and goblets and believed that wine tasted differently depending on the colour of the glass from which it was drunk. The dining room and bar have the planned economy of a galley, but some largeness of gesture, perhaps the exuberant size of some of the glasses, saves the whole from any constricting sense of tightness and neatness.

Across a small courtyard a winding staircase leads into a circular sitting room with lavish leather chairs and several sculptures. Chile was in the middle of a prolonged drought with an electricity and water crisis while we were there. The Mapocho River that runs through Santiago was reduced to a thin trickle and in places the riverbed showed nothing but dusty pebbles and boulders. Nevertheless, I couldn't help wondering what it would be like to have to cross from cabin to cabin on a rainy day or during a semi-tropical downpour.

The fullest section of La Chascona, which was built in 1955, is the large study-library which stands by itself in the far corner of the garden. It is a beautifully organised room with a high window looking down over the city (It can be no accident that this house is situated in the Bellavista area). The library here is the most complete of all the houses and now contains all of Neruda's books that have survived. We were not allowed to take any photographs inside the rooms, only in the gardens. I hope that was because the foundation has plans for a future in postcards or photographic volumes and wants to protect its copyright, and not for security reasons. I noticed on the shelves handsome early editions of the complete works of Melville and Poe, Whitman and Conrad. There were sets of the major nineteenth-century French poets, Baudelaire, Rimbaud, Mallarmé and Lautréamont in their white Pléiade jackets and celluloid covers. In his early student days Neruda planned to be a teacher of French. He spent some important years in Paris and there are various signs throughout his houses of his great love of French art and literature, photos, postcards, prints and maps. The books in his library looked as if they had been well used and were not just possessions on display, though some of the sets may well have been acquired in his later more affluent days in homage to admired authors. There was an impressive mappemonde-globe resting on a long table, perhaps a late reproduction item and probably acquired by Neruda in his travels.

A small room off the front office was lined with photographs, giving a biographical outline of the main dates and events of Neruda's life – photos from his early consular years in Java, Singapore, Rangoon, Colombo, Barcelona, Madrid, Buenos Aires, Mexico; his years in exile, meetings with Federico García Lorca and Paul Éluard. We were in Santiago while Pinochet was still under house arrest in England waiting extradition to Spain and there was wide-spread speculation on how the case would develop. One Chilean woman said to me 'Sure, bad things were done in the past but we want to forget about all that and move on. Pinochet is now a very old man'. The democratic elections that were to bring Ricardo Lagos to power had not yet been held though we witnessed a number of street parades and demonstrations supporting him and there was already a palpable sense of change and freedom in the air. But standing in that small room which outlined the main dates and events of Neruda's life, I noticed that all mention of his association with the Communist Party and with Allende's regime had been omitted, as had the fact that he had received various prestigious prizes and awards from Eastern Europe during the Cold War (including the Stalin Prize for Peace and Friendship among Peoples) before the Nobel Prize for Literature came to him in 1971. Perhaps this was part of a calculated attempt to defuse him politically during the Pinochet years or to guarantee the establishment of the Neruda houses on a non-political and totally independent footing. Neruda is a great national poet, the modern lyrical-epic poet of Chile, and this particular display seemed anxious to focus on the poet rather than the political figure.

A few days later we were in Valparaíso, a place I have longed to see since my school days in Hobart and to which so many of the merchant ships which passed through that once busy port seemed to be heading. As we drove towards the coast I was often reminded of parts of Tasmania and outback New South Wales, not only by the eucalyptus trees that South America owes to us, as we owe it our jacaranda trees, but even by some of the small country and seaside towns we passed through, as well as the hills, the light and the sky.

La Sebastiana, the house above Valparaíso that Neruda started building in 1959, is the most impressive of all his residences, and the one that suffered most from looting and vandalism at the time of the takeover by the Pinochet military dictatorship. It too has a superb position high above the great port and harbour and the waters of the South Pacific, and it holds something of the atmospheres of a large lighthouse, a lookout and a fort. It now has a carefully tended garden, pebbled pathways, neat clipped sections of lawn and beautiful tropical plants along with cacti, succulents and native shrubs. Just to one side of the path to the main entrance is a metal seat, a chaise longue in fact, with a silhouette profile of Neruda cut into the back where one can sit and have a photo taken, facing towards the poet as though in conversation.

It would be easy to think that having visited one Neruda house, one has seen them all. They have many features in common: their ground plans seem to be much the same, the sailing ship atmosphere, bars that look and feel like ships' cabins, and they all display wonderful collections of various kinds – shells and butterflies, model ships in bottles, glassware, wine glasses, primitive and colonial South American paintings. But it would be a mistake to merge them all together. Each house has its own unique design and shape, its own slightly different atmosphere and features, and each has very individual variations on basic themes. La Chascona has the city of Santiago and the orange-grey Andes mountains in the background; La Sebastiana looks from on high out across the city and the harbour of Valparaíso and it makes a greater impression of size and airiness. It is a real house, a home, rather than a pied-à-terre. Like its companions, it was lived in before it became a museum, and each house has its particular place in Neruda's biography. Presumably because of its position, it was the house where Neruda had planned a landing stage for space ships. Devotee of science fiction, Poe and Verne and visionary Rimbaud, he was convinced that interplanetary travel would be a feature of the future and a rudimentary outline for a landing pad or a space for such a development is indicated in one of the upstairs rooms. This may well have been one of Neruda's broad jokes but we were told it in all seriousness by the guide who led us around.

Valparaíso itself must be one of the most amazing places in the world. Its haunting name – with its touch of Paradise – suggests how it must have appeared to its first discoverers. Although it is now the administrative and parliamentary capital of Chile, it is an old port and it has some of the aspects of a shantytown, having become rundown and neglected in the upheavals of recent years. It is a steeply sloped place of colourful wooden houses, chalets and villas with long glassed in verandahs and balconies. But with its tiers of weatherboard houses, many of the most fanciful shapes, some of Swiss and Austrian alpine designs, it must once have been extraordinarily beautiful and striking. Many of the once-superb old houses now look derelict and worm-eaten, ready to blow away in dust and flames, while the more recent stand out in stone and concrete. The great harbour should ideally be full of sailing ships, barques, brigantines, four-masted clippers, whalers and windjammers; but it still makes a very busy and lively impression with its yachts, fishing boats, barges, frigates, tugs, trawlers, container ships, freighters and warships of the Chilean navy.

Like the other houses, La Sebastiana, now fully restored, shows further additions to Neruda's principal collections of a lifetime: more glass, more paintings, seascapes and still lifes, a vitrine full of scrimshaw, a couple of ships' figureheads which reminded me of those that used to be on display and for sale in Patmore's secondhand furniture shop up Liverpool Street in Hobart when I lived there during the early 1950s; a marvellous old rocking horse, crocheted quilts on old-fashioned iron bedsteads with brass knobs. One room displayed a series of nineteenth century prints of Africa, Asia, Europe and America and an impressive collection of old maps of the world, maritime charts and nautical instruments which reminded me of the imagery of Kenneth Slessor, a poet who has more in common with writers like Neruda and Borges than is often realised.

From one wall a huge photographic blow-up of Walt Whitman surveyed the room with a look of shrewd benevolence, gazing towards the door that was supposed to open on to those future journeys to the stars. Standing in these rooms with their photographs and postcards of Rimbaud and Lautréamont I again saw the importance they had in Neruda's imaginative world: '*le Bateau Ivre*' seemed to outline the journey of Neruda's life, and Lautréamont, having been born, like Laforgue, in Montevideo, must have had a special significance for him as a South American.

As well as journeys to the stars, Neruda, the guide told us, planned to establish an aviary here, perhaps a kind of sanctuary, which would hold specimens of all the birds of the world. Like Judith Wright, Neruda loved their colours and shapes, and he greatly regretted the disappearance of so many different species. Now the room holds only the embalmed scarlet form of a rare Venezuelan bird that swings from the ceiling in a transparent perspex envelope.

As in most National Heritage set-ups around the world, there are rooms which are simply not open to the public, kitchens and bathrooms in particular, but there was evidence enough elsewhere that Neruda, celebrant of cooking and the dinner table, was a considerable collector of domestic objects, kitchen- and tableware, plates and cups and saucers and soup tureens, whole dinner sets in fact, as well as of bathroom accessories such as florally decorated porcelain washbasins and handbasins and lavatory bowls. There were a few solid items of French provenance standing around among the bric-a-brac, like Duchamp ready-mades: obviously never installed for use, just collected and kept, perhaps they had been waiting for their moment to inspire an Ode to a *Pot de chambre* or a Hymn to a Bidet.

Once again there was the bar with cocktail cabinet and rows and rows of coloured glasses and goblets; in the bedroom a woman's shoes, dresses in a wardrobe, leather armchairs and a fireplace designed by Neruda himself though built by an architect. One room was devoted to a series of photographs covering the time of Neruda's exile in Capri.

Like Neruda's houses, the city of Valparaíso also makes a very eclectic impression. Strong German and Yugoslav (especially Croatian) influences are visible in the designs and shapes of the houses and our minibus stopped briefly in front of a German-style stone and cement house with swastikas set into the wall above the entrance and a couple of Alsatian dogs prowling in the grounds. It was hard to know what to make of this. Was it some pre-war manifestation of local support for Hitler or some kind of post-war defiance? So much has been written about former Nazis escaping to and hiding in various parts of South America that our alarm bells inadvertently started ringing. My knowledge of the history of Chile is limited to a tourist smattering but it is quite clear from many surnames in public life that the German presence has been long established in the Southern Cone.

Apart from a few Easter Island artefacts or imitations of them, Neruda does not seem to have collected any pre-Columbian items at all; no older native or indigenous items were visible. Much of his life, apart from his years in the East, was centred in Europe, where most of the elements in his various collections were assembled. When it came to South American objects, I had the impression that his collector's interest focused mainly on seventeenth- and eighteenth-century colonial items: maps, still-lives, primitive and maritime paintings, insects and seashells, and that these were supplemented by substantial collections of dolls, toys and games from all round the world.

My wife and I had flown to Santiago after spending ten days in Buenos Aires and we had been immediately struck by the differences between the two countries whose capitals we liked so much. Buenos Aires is modern and cosmopolitan, a predominantly nineteenth- and twentieth-century city, something like a mixture of Paris and New York, looking towards Europe across the Atlantic. We happened to be there during the centenary celebrations of Jorge Luis Borges, that most European of Argentine writers, whose familiar face was featured in all the marvellous bookshops in Avenidas Corrientes and Florida together with the various new editions of his work. There is a Borges path or walk from his former apartment in Calle Maipú around the different Borges sites, and the Centro Cultural Borges put on a fine exhibition of photographs and editions.

Santiago on the other hand looks towards the Pacific, Polynesia, New Zealand and Tasmania. There are more Indian faces in the street and a manifest indigenous political presence. Santiago looks less prosperous than Buenos Aires and more rural and agricultural. One afternoon we saw a man leading a donkey down a footpath of the Avenida del Libertador

General Bernardo O'Higgins not far from the CBD; it carried a double bag of cactus fruit on its back. The Spanish-Catholic colonial heritage is much more vividly present in churches and museums than anything we saw in Argentina.

After three days of long and leisurely exploration around Santiago – the wonderful Franciscan monastery and museum, the markets and the magnificent old Mapocho railway station, now turned like the Quai d'Orsay and other similar places around the world into heritage sites – we decided to make another organised trip to the coast to see another Neruda monument, this time his house at Isla Negra – the oldest of all his houses, the first one he acquired in 1939 and the one he seems to have lived in the longest and referred to most often in his poetry and prose. Our fellow travellers on this excursion were a young American couple, he of Pennsylvanian German background studying to be a Lutheran pastor and teaching English to Spanish students. We had gone on the only available daytrip as part of a small bus group led by an American pilot who had lived in Chile since 1963. He told us he was married to a Chilean and that he had lost his job when Allende nationalised the airlines. He had nothing but praise for Pinochet and the Pinochet years which, he said, had brought unprecedented prosperity to the country.

'The military government improved everything.

If you didn't stir up trouble, you didn't get into trouble'. He was not pleased when I said I wanted to visit Neruda's house at Isla Negra though the Lutheran knew the poet's work and spoke highly of it: 'Neruda, that old whisky-drinking commo – had the best of everything for himself'. I heard him say something about 'womaniser, best suits made overseas, best whisky... everything went to his friends in Cuba and Russia', but I couldn't tell at that stage if he was talking about Neruda or Allende. Later he said that the stories about the disappeared ones were just bits of myth. 'All of the commos went into exile after Allende turned the machine gun on himself. They knew they would never have it so good again. They are the disappeared ones; they fled the country.' After a while his diatribe trailed off and we concentrated on the vineyards, the orchards and the market gardens that sped by and then the huge windswept places along the coast – Cartegena, San Antonio, San Jose, fashionable seaside resorts in summer.

Isla Negra differs from Neruda's other two houses in that it is situated directly on the sea, overlooking nothing but a long stretch of rocky ironstone coast and the vast waters of the Pacific. I had always thought it must be a promontory or a small island close to shore but it is in fact part of the mainland resembling many similar seaside places in Australia, just hidden and isolated from the main road by a slope and a turning. It is here that Neruda lies buried, his grave in the garden facing the huge swell of the sea and the immense grey and blue of the sky. Part of the main house looks like an Australian seaside shack, but the whole compound is solidly constructed out of stones and protected by a severe wall and iron gates. If it suffered depredations and vandalising like the other houses after the fall of the Allende government – it was closed to all access by the Pinochet military for some years – it has now been carefully restored and renovated and a couple of new annexes seem to have been built to display the various collections to best advantage.

Isla Negra was the place that Neruda seems to have been most attached to; it was originally his writer's getaway and is the most isolated of all his houses. It was the subject of a fine book edited by Sara Facio of photographs taken in the last years of his life, but perhaps because a number of the more private rooms were not open to the public, it made a less personal impression than the book evoked. One section suggests a room in a natural history museum, which is of course what it has in a way become. But all the houses also make a slightly fantastic impression, like pieces of strange surrealist sculpture. 'This man had no taste', a young German tourist said to me, 'he was weird'. And while this reaction was far from being mine, I could see where it was coming from.

As with the other houses, a sense of order

and careful organisation reigns. We are in a supervised cultural monument now but it isn't hard to imagine the convivial life, the meetings and the wining and the dining with so many friends and visitors that must have taken place there during Neruda's lifetime. Wandering in the garden and on the shore where his face is carved on a rock, I reflected that while two of Neruda's favourite poets – Baudelaire and Mallarmé – are associated with cats, mirrors and interiors, it seems appropriate that he should have been a dog lover and associated with horses, mountains and the sea.

It turned into a rather cold and blustering day, the weather intermittently wet and wild. Perhaps we had reached a saturation point in our travels; perhaps something of our tour guide's hostility to the changes that were in the Chilean air had started to seep in and gave the visit a touch of haste and unfriendliness. I felt I needed much more time to look around and absorb things than we were allowed. There were more objects and collections crowded here than in the other houses and less time to give to them. In one room there was a life-sized papier-mâché horse looking so real that I assumed that it was a stuffed carcass until better informed. Isla Negra has the finest of Neruda's collections of insects – beetles, spiders, dung beetles – and a case of enormous Brazilian butterflies – as well as of seashells. Indeed seashells seem to have been for Neruda what butterflies were for Nabokov.

He collected them and bought them throughout his lifetime and while many of them, according to his *Memoirs*, have been lost, all his houses contain great numbers and varieties. His largest collection of toys, ships' figureheads, anchors, bells, ships in bottles and miniature musical instruments (mostly guitars and mandolins) are here as well as a huge array of glass jars, bottles and intricate glass paperweights. In the garden with its windbitten succulents and sturdy picket fence on the edge of the beach an old locomotive engine stands abandoned amid small native palms and agaves. A huge ship's bell swings from a post.

There is a sense of opulence in all of Neruda's houses, even of self-indulgence, but the collections are idiosyncratic rather than ostentatious and most of the objects seemed to have been picked up over the years at markets and fairs. Whatever their value now, they were obviously acquired at a time when such objects could have been obtained for very little money and because they interested and were liked and enjoyed by the poet himself. They were not bought to be resold or for financial gain but to be left to his country like his houses, one of which at least was intended as a writers' retreat or centre.

Neruda's houses are potentially the most surrealistic I have seen. The many varied objects in them could provide material for some startling juxtapositions, something rarer and more daring than a sewing machine and an umbrella meeting on a dissecting table, the provocation of a lobster telephone or the disorientation of a clam playing an accordion. But such contrivances belong more to the realm of fancy and fantasy and they would be out of keeping with the robust, essentially practical, almost nautical, atmosphere that prevails. In Neruda's houses everything remains basically down to earth and rooted in this world just as it does in his poetry.

Note

The Real Life of Ern Malley: The Ern Malley *cause célèbre* has been a feature of Australian literary life since 1944 and interest in it has waxed and waned over the years. It found a new lease of life with a generation of writers and academics born after the event itself when they learned of the impact it had had on John Ashbery and a number of other writers overseas. In the meantime there had been several reissues of the Ern Malley poems and various studies of the poems themselves. The 1974 edition of *The Darkening Ecliptic*, edited by Elwyn Lynn, is particularly valuable, as is the post-mortem number of *Angry Penguins*, December 1944.

Some material in this sequence was suggested by books by Michael Heyward, Cassandra Pybus and Michael Ackland, as well as *The Diaries of Donald Friend*, but my main source has been the Ern Malley paintings of Sidney Nolan.

I was lucky enough to meet most of the people caught up in the Ern Malley affair, and to know some of them quite well.